W9-CEG-273

Growing Readers

New Hanover County Public Library

Purchased with
New Hanover County Partnership for Children
and Smart Start Funds

Let's Make Tacos

By Mary Hill

Children's Press®
A Division of Scholastic Inc.
New York / Toronto / London / Auckland / Sydney
Mexico City / New Delhi / Hong Kong
Danbury, Connecticut

NEW HANOVER COUNTY
PUBLIC LIBRARY
201 CHESTNUT STREET
WILMINGTON, NC 28401

Photo Credits: Cover and all photos by Maura B. McConnell
Contributing Editor: Jennifer Silate
Book Design: Mindy Liu

Library of Congress Cataloging-in-Publication Data

Hill, Mary, 1977-
Let's make tacos / by Mary Hill.
    p. cm. — (In the kitchen)
  Includes index.
  Summary: A boy and his mother demonstrate the steps involved in making
  tacos.
  ISBN 0-516-23957-0 (lib. bdg.) — ISBN 0-516-24021-8 (pbk.)
  1. Tacos—Juvenile literature. [1. Tacos.] I. Title.

TX836 .H55 2002
641.8—dc21

                                                          2002004869

Copyright © 2002 by Rosen Book Works, Inc.
All rights reserved. Published simultaneously in Canada.
Printed in the United States of America.
1 2 3 4 5 6 7 8 9 10 R 11 10 09 08 07 06 05 04 03 02

Contents

My name is Dean.

Mom and I are making **tacos**.

TACO
SEASONING MIX

TACO CHEESE

5

Mom cooks some meat in a **pan**.

She adds **spices** to make the meat taste good.

I wash the tomatoes.

I make sure that they are clean.

Mom cuts the tomatoes into small **pieces**.

We put everything
into bowls.

13

It is time to eat!

First, I put meat in my **taco shell**.

Next, I put cheese in my taco shell.

I put the cheese on top of the meat.

Finally, I put some tomatoes in my taco.

My taco is finished.

It tastes good.

New Words

pan (**pan**) a wide, shallow container that is used for cooking

pieces (**peess**-ez) bits of something larger

spices (**spisse**-ez) things used to flavor foods

tacos (**tah**-kohz) fried tortilla that is folded around one or more fillings, such as beef or cheese

taco shell (**tah**-koh **shel**) a folded, fried tortilla

To Find Out More

Books

Cool Kids Cook
by Donna Hay
Whitecap Books

The Kids' Multicultural Cookbook
by Deanna F. Cook
Williamson Publishing

Web Site

Cookalotamus Kids
http://www.cookalotamus.com
Play games, print out pictures to color, and find delicious recipes on this fun Web site.

Index

About the Author

Mary Hill writes and edits children's books from her home in Maryland.

Reading Consultants

Kris Flynn, Coordinator, Small School District Literacy, The San Diego County Office of Education

Shelly Forys, Certified Reading Recovery Specialist, W.J. Zahnow Elementary School, Waterloo, IL

Sue McAdams, Former President of the North Texas Reading Council of the IRA, and Early Literacy Consultant, Dallas, TX

24

Growing Readers
New Hanover County Public Library
201 Chestnut Street
Wilmington, NC 28401